'A STAB IN THE HEART'

by

MIKE WILSON

Illustrations:	Jim Harmes
Layout:	Julia Holt
Editing:	Peter Beynon

NEWMAT

ALBSU
Adult Literacy & Basic Skills Unit

Produced by NEWMAT – A Special Development Project
for Nottinghamshire County Council, funded by ALBSU.

Published May 1988

ISBN 1 871174 13 9

Contents

Nick Mason

Lola

Blade Raines

J.T. Morgan

Johnny Wing

4

Doctor Mansfield

Rico

Ann Hammond

The Editor

The Chief of Police

After The Party

The man from the newspaper
took one more look around the room.
Then he started to write in his note book.

It must have been quite a party!
Empty glasses. Broken bottles.
Ash trays – dead cigarettes.
Dead smoke in the air.

Lights on, curtains shut.
Living room, tiny kitchen.

3 bedrooms – all slept in.
Quite a party!!

The girl was lying on the sofa.
Her mouth was open, but her eyes were shut.
She looked peaceful.
One arm hung towards the floor.
She was long, blonde, and pretty —
very pretty.

But the knife in her back wasn't pretty.
It was cheap and ugly.
She had been dead for about ten hours.
That's what the detective said —
and he was the expert.

"I think maybe she was a good time girl,"
the detective was saying.
"I think she went to a lot of parties…"
He rubbed his chin, and looked over at the reporter.
"What do *you* think, Nick?"

"Maybe," said Nick. "Who owns this place, Jack?"
"We don't know," said the detective. "Could be her?"
"No," said Nick. "It's a nice quiet place, out of town. Too classy."
"Yes, right. Maybe she had a sugar-daddy."
"Anyhow, you'll have to find out who *she* was first," said Nick.

"Look!" said the detective.
"These scars on her wrist.
They should be a good clue..."

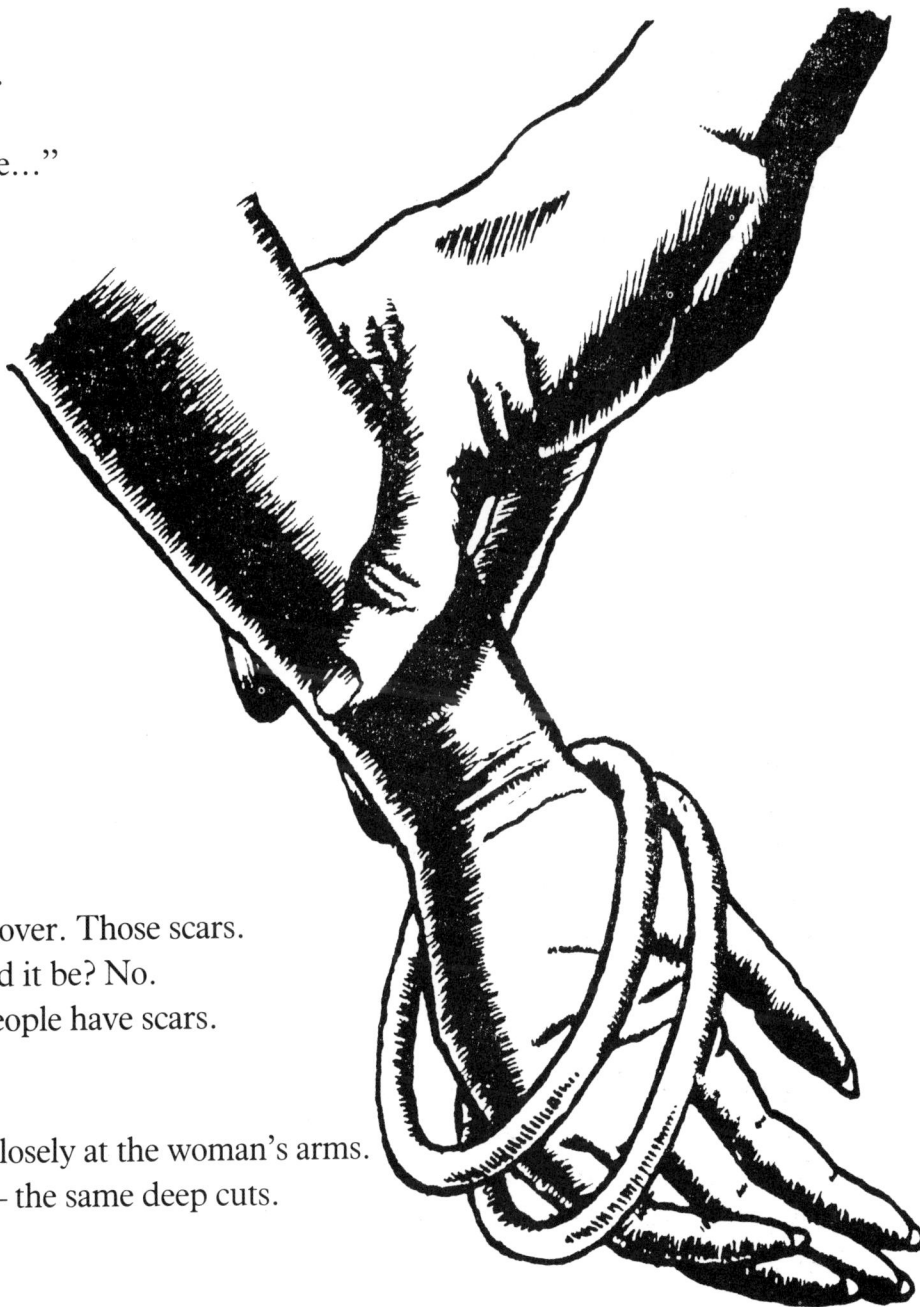

Nick felt his stomach turn over. Those scars.
His mind went back. Could it be? No.
Don't be stupid. Lots of people have scars.
It could be anyone.

He went over and looked closely at the woman's arms.
The scars were the same — the same deep cuts.
Two on each wrist.
Oh God! He felt sick.

9

"I wonder who she was...." the detective was saying.

"Her name....was....Ann Hammond," Nick said slowly.
"I didn't recognise her. She wasn't a blonde when I knew her."

He bent down and stroked the dead woman's hair.
He pulled gently and it came away in his hand.
It was a wig.
Underneath, her hair was short and light brown.
She looked strange and naked
without the blonde wig.
Suddenly she looked beautiful.

The Editor

Nick's editor was angry. But then he was always angry.

"Why can't you tell me how you know this woman?"
Nick said nothing.

"I give up!" the editor shouted.
He jabbed a finger at Nick.
"You're off the story," he said.
"I'm getting someone else to cover it."

"No boss, I'm the man for the job.
I know the case. I knew the victim.
I can make a really good story of it —
just give me a couple of days."

The editor frowned. He stared long and hard at Nick.
He looked as if he had a bad taste in his mouth.
"Alright," he said.
"You've got till Friday. Now get going."

Nick smiled. "Thanks boss," he said.
The phone rang as Nick left the office.

Five minutes later, the editor called him back.
"What's up, boss?" he asked.
"The case is closed. The cops have got the killer —
a waiter at the party. They picked him up this afternoon.
He killed her for money, or something.

"That doesn't add up," said Nick. "She...."
"Look, you're off the story Nick," the editor shouted.
"How many times do I have to tell you? You're off this story!"

Nick could see the editor was scared.
Somebody had phoned and told him to lay off.
Somebody big —
someone important.
But who?
"O.K., boss, O.K. You win," Nick said with a shrug.
He left the editor's office and went back to his desk.

Nick was going to ignore the order.
He had to find out who the killer was.
For Ann's sake.
He had phone calls to make.

13

J.T. Morgan and Johnny Wing

A waiter was in jail for killing Ann Hammond.
Nick knew he didn't do it.

He went to see J.T. Morgan, the man's lawyer.
They met in a dirty little office in a dirty part of town.
J.T. Morgan wore sunglasses, all the time, even
indoors.
Nick couldn't see his eyes.

"I'm from 'The Herald'," said Nick.
"I know your man is being framed.
But that's all I know.
Tell me how can I help."
J.T. looked him up and down,
from behind his dark glasses.
He nodded slowly,
but Nick knew he was thinking fast.

Then J.T. started to tell Nick the story.
"The man in jail is Johnny Wing.
He works in a Chinese Restaurant,
out near the house where the woman died.

14

Sometimes he delivered food for the parties there.
He made a delivery on the night of the murder.
But he was only there a minute."

"How many meals did he take?" asked Nick.
"Only three, but that doesn't tell you anything.
Not everyone was eating."
"How many people did he see?"
"Six or seven women.
You know — the sort who have a day-time job,
but work at night as well...."

Nick thought about Ann.
What was she doing
in a place like that?"
He didn't want to think about it.
"What about the men?"
he asked.

15

"Four" said the lawyer.
"But Johnny didn't get a good look at them.
There was a fat man, a thin man,
an old man and a good-looking guy.
The good-looking guy — Johnny knew him —
he'd seen him before."

Nick sat up. "Who was it?"

"His name is Blade Raines. A bit part actor.
Johnny Wing had seen him in the movies."

They talked some more. Then Nick stood up.
"I'd better be going," he said.
"There's no time to lose."
Nick walked to the door.

"Why are you doing this?" asked J.T.
"Johnny Wing is nothing to you.
Is it the girl?"

Nick looked back at the man in shades.
Quietly, he said,
"That's another story."

A Beginning

Six years ago. Another world. Another story.

The lift was out of order, so Nick went up the stairs.
They were dark, and damp,
and they smelled of the usual things.

He rang the bell on the door marked 409.
But he knew there would be no answer.

A crazy old lady had lived there.
She had died the week before.
All she left was a sad old dog, crying in the night.
The paper wanted a story about the poor old dog,
left all alone.

"Jesus," Nick said to himself.
"This is sick.
What am I doing here?"

He went next door, to Number 408.
He rang twice.

The door opened a few inches.
A woman looked out.
"What the hell do you want?"

Nick leaned on the wall.
"Do you want to see your name in the papers?
Tell me about the old girl next door —
the one with the dog."

"Who, Alice?" The woman didn't believe him.
"Why?"

"I want to make some people cry," said Nick.

They went over to a bar —
and drank coffee for an hour.
She told him about the crazy old woman
and her crazy old dog.
The howling had kept her awake at night.
Then someone had come and taken the dog away.

Then, Nick stood up.
"Is that it?" she asked.
"Yes," he said. "I have to go now."
"Is that all?" She wanted him to stay.
"That's all," he said.

"When will I be in the paper?"
"Tomorrow. Maybe Monday."
"I'd like....we could go....for a drink.....
sometime...." she said. "A real drink."
"Maybe," said Nick. "Yes, why not?"
"How about tonight?" she smiled.
Nick smiled back.

"O.K. Sure," he said, and turned to go.
"You haven't even asked my name!"
she called after him.
"Tell me."
"Ann," she said, "Ann Hammond."

The Picture

It was late.
Nick was back in his office.
Everyone else had gone home.
The room was full of newspapers.
There was a pile on his desk,
and he was going quickly through every page.
He was looking for something.
Or someone.

When he finished with one,
he threw it away.
It flapped and fell like a dead bird,
then lay on the floor with the others.

At last Nick found it.
He sat back staring at the picture.
Two men looked back at him.
They were sitting at a table in a night-club.
Around them were bright lights and pretty girls.

He read:
"Actor Blade Raines dining out last night
at *"LOLA'S"* Night-Club.
There was a party for Lola's birthday.
Blade's latest film...."

Nick looked back at the picture.
The man with Raines was fat.
And his hair was full of oil.
Eyes like snakes — quick and dangerous.
He looked angry. He didn't want his picture taken.
He didn't want his face in the papers.

Blade Raines looked smooth and cool.
He had charm.
He was the wrong side of 40,
but he was smiling like a school-boy.

"I don't like him." Nick said to himself.
"I don't like the look of him.
He's too good-looking."

And what was he doing at *"LOLA'S"*?
The joint was full of hoods,
not the sort of place for movie actors.
And who was the fat man?
Where did he fit in?

Nick looked at his watch — midnight.
Lola's would be coming to life.
Maybe he should go down there
and ask some questions.

Nick ripped the picture out of the newspaper,
and left the office without turning off the light.

"Lola's"

Lola took the cigarette from her red lips, and blew smoke into Nick's face.

"Yes," she said, "I know Blade Raines, I know lots of people."

They were sitting in her office in the night-club.
There was a big two-way mirror in the wall,
and they could see onto the dance floor next door.
Everyone was drinking and dancing and having a good time.
But no noise came through to the office.
Nick sat there, looking at Lola,
and there wasn't a sound in the room.

He took out a photo of Ann
and dropped it on Lola's lap.
He had taken it six years ago,
down at the beach,
when Ann was happy and alive.

"Where did you get this?" Lola asked.
"This woman died last night," he said.
"It's a big bad world," said Lola after a while.
"Did you know her?"
"I may have seen her in here a few times…"
Nick knew she was lying.
"Was she one of your girls?"
"I don't *have* girls. It's not that kind of place, mister."
But Nick knew that it was.

24

He gave her the picture from the paper
of Blade Raines and the fat man at the club.
"Who's the fat guy?" he asked.
"Look mister," she said,
"I like you. Do yourself a favour.
Stay away from him. He's bad news."

"What's his name?"
Lola took a drag on her cigarette.
She leaned back and blew the smoke up into the air.
"Rico. Everyone calls him Rico."

"What does he do?"
"I don't know....this and that.
He buys and sells....things.
I don't know...."

Nick could see that Lola knew a lot more,
but she wasn't going to say.
She was scared, like his editor.

They sat in silence,
looking at one another.
The dancers moved slowly past the window.
"Just like big stupid fish," thought Nick.

Suddenly the phone rang and Lola jumped.
She picked it up and listened.
"Not now....No, not here....
I can't....O.K. Just wait....
Where are you? I'll be right there."
She hung up.

Lola went to the door.
"I'm sorry, Mr Mason."
"Call me Nick."
"I have to leave now. You stay here.
Have a drink on the house."

Nick took her arm.
"Before you go," he said.
"Who do *you* think killed her?"

Lola laughed softly and shook her arm free.
Her red lips curled into a sort of smile.
"It's a man's world, Nick," she said.
"Men killed her."

The House

Nick waited at the bar until Lola had gone.
Then he went out to his car.
Lola was driving fast,
heading out of town in a cloud of dust.
As soon as she was out of sight,
Nick started his car.

He didn't need to follow her.
He knew where she was going.
And he knew that somehow
Rico was mixed up
in this crazy mess.

27

He parked in the lane,
half a mile from the house where Ann had died,
and walked the rest of the way in the shadows.
Lights were on in the house,
and he could see Lola's car parked outside.

Two men were taking boxes from the house,
and were loading them into Lola's car.

One of them had a limp —
the sort of limp you get
when a bullet hits you in the leg.

They were working quickly.
Nick checked the time.
It was nearly 2.00 am.

Then 'The Limp' dropped a box.
A bag of white powder fell out
and burst open.

'The Limp' bent down stiffly
to save what he could.

Nick crept round to the back of the house.
He hid in the shadow of a wall.
There was a fire burning in the garden,
and Nick could see Lola.

She was dropping something into the flames.
Papers....letters....an address book?
A man came out.
It was the fat man —
Rico.

Nick was so close
that he could hear every word.
They were talking about him!

"He had a picture of Ann," Lola was saying.
"I don't know where he got it."

"No-one has seen Blade today," Rico said.
"We must find him,
before he opens his big mouth."
He poked at the fire with a stick.

Nick heard a car pull up in front of the house.
Another man came out into the garden.
He walked over to the fire,
and dropped in some reels of film.

"Burn it all," he said.

Nick held his breath.
The button on the man's uniform
glinted in the firelight.
Nick knew his face.
It was The Chief of Police.

30

The Chief of Police

The Chief of Police was angry.
He couldn't keep still.
He was shaking with rage.
The reels of film began to hiss
and crackle in the fire.

He strode over to Rico
and slapped him hard across the face.
"You fool!" he shouted.
"You stupid fat bungling God-damn fool!"
Rico said nothing.
He put his hand to his face
and made a whining noise like a little puppy.

"I had to get my men out of this house today,"
said the Chief,
"in case they found all this stuff
and traced it back to me.
A Police Chief who takes men *off* the case!
Huh!"
He spat and swore.

31

Rico looked at his feet.
"Sorry boss," he mumbled.

The Chief looked at Lola.
"Beat it, Lola.
Take the stuff and get the hell out.
Just like I told you.
Now!"
Lola left without saying a word.

Then he turned to Rico.
"O.K. Rico. What happened last night?"
Who killed Ann Hammond?"

"I don't know, Boss.
She was talking to Blade Raines.
Blade was waiting for Dr Mansfield.
After Blade got his stuff, he left.
Ann went with him.
She took my spare key to this place," Rico went on.
"I didn't know it was gone till later.
So she must have let herself back in —
after the party."

"O.K. She met someone later," said The Police Chief.
"And *that* person —
whoever it was —
killed her."
He rubbed his chin and stared into the fire.

"Blade Raines knows something —
and he'll talk for sure.
He's nothing but a damned fool.
Rico — we gotta shut him up.
For keeps."

"O.K. Boss, but there's something else."
"What?" barked The Chief.
"A reporter…….."
"I've fixed him, Rico," said The Chief.
"I called his Editor today. He won't bother us."

"But he was round at Lola's tonight.
Asking all sorts of questions."

The Chief went very quiet and still.
Then he said,
"So we'll have to shut *him* up too…."

Nick crept back to his car.

On the way home,
he tried to fit the pieces together.

Ann and Blade Raines
were in on something together.
They were waiting for some doctor....

Was Blade sick?
Or was he after something else?
And how did Ann fit in?

Who did she meet after the party?
Was it Blade — did *he* kill her?
If not, he might know who did.
The Chief of Police was worried.
He was going to shut Blade's mouth.

Nick had to see Blade.
But it was 2.45 am.
He'd have to wait a few hours.

Nick couldn't go home —
The Chief was after him too.

Nick turned his car off the road.
He pulled his hat over his eyes
and tried to get some sleep.

34

Blade Raines

Nick woke at dawn.
He drove to an all-night diner,
and had coffee and a scotch.

He knew the kind of hotels where Blade Raines stayed.
He phoned around.
He got lucky with his third call.
The desk clerk put him through.

Blade Raines should have sounded sleepy,
but he didn't.
He was wide awake and on his guard.
Nick was sure there was someone with him.

Nick said,
"I'm Nick Mason from 'The Herald'.
I'd like to do an interview with you.
Right away."

Blade said: "One moment."
Nick heard another voice
but Blade must have put his hand over the phone —

Nick couldn't hear what they said.
Suddenly Blade was back.
"That's perfect. Be here in half an hour.

Nick hung up and went out to his car.

Who was Blade Raines talking to?
Why did he say "That's perfect"?
Nick had a feeling
he was walking into a trap.

When Nick got to Blade's hotel room.
Blade was waiting at the door.
"So kind of you to come," he smiled.
"Welcome!" He waved an arm grandly in the air.

"You may be a good actor," Nick was thinking,
but you don't fool me."

When they were inside, Nick said:
"Let's talk about Ann Hammond, Mr Raines...."

"Ah," said Blade Raines.
"Yes, I heard about Bracelets.
So sad....poor thing....so sad."
"Why did you call her Bracelets, Mr Raines?"

"She wore them all the time, the darling," he said
smoothly.
"It was our little joke.
She was such *fun* you know, Nick."

He put an arm around Nick's shoulder,
as if they were the best of friends.

The room was full of hats, masks and costumes.
All over the walls were photos of plays and film posters.
Blade Raines was in all of them.
His face looked at Nick from every angle,
and it was always different,
and always the same.

BLADE RAINES

He led Nick over to a table in the corner
and picked up a silver cigarette case.
"Do you smoke, dear boy?" he said,
holding out a silver lighter.

It was such a good act, Nick fell for it.

He bent over the flame —
and then there was a splitting pain
in the back of his head.
Nick was sure one of the photos on the wall
had come to life, and hit him.
Or shot him, he couldn't tell.

He stood for a second, swaying, seeing stars.
staring blindly at the smiling actor,
with the flame still in his hand.

It was the last thing Nick saw.
He crumpled up and fell in a heap.
The darkness slammed down on him
like the lid of a coffin.

Wanted for Murder

The pain just wouldn't go away.

Someone was hitting Nick on the head with a hammer.
Then, after a while, the hammering was on the inside.
It was telling him to wake up, and open his eyes.
He did.

He was lucky to be alive.
He knew that.
He just didn't feel it.

He was lying on his back in Blade's hotel room.
He was holding a gun in his right hand.
He lifted it up.
He'd never seen it before.

Slowly, Nick turned his head.
Blade Raines was lying next to him,
staring into Nick's face,
but he wasn't seeing anything.
And he wasn't smiling any more.
Someone had made him promise
to keep a secret.

Now Nick could see how The Chief of Police
had planned to shut him up.
He was going to throw Nick in jail
for murdering Blade.
That way, both Blade and Nick
would be shut up for ever.

Nick had to act fast.
He got up,
and put the gun in his pocket.

Then he went over to the window.
There was a fire escape,
leading down to a back alley.

He got out of the window
and went down the rusty steps.
When he got to the ground
he hid in a door way.
He tried to think.

I'm a wanted man.
I'm on the run.
They'll be looking for me everywhere.
I can't go home.
I can't use my car.
I have no money.
I can't trust anyone.

He could think of only one place
where he might be safe for a while.
The last place
that the police would think to look.

Nick walked out of the alley
and lost himself in the crowd.
As far as he could tell
nobody followed him.

41

Chapter 11 : Thursday 8.30 pm

A Sort of Love

Lola got to the club at 8.30 that night.
When she let herself in,
Nick was sitting at the desk in her office.
Her address book was open on the desk.

For a moment she was surprised,
but she hid it well.
She even seemed pleased to see him.

She put two cigarettes in her mouth,
and lit them.
She put one between Nick's lips.
"What are you doing here?" she asked coolly.

"I broke in," said Nick.
"I'll pay for the window.
I had nowhere else to go.
Blade is dead."

"Dead?" Lola went white and stared at Nick.

"Rico and The Police Chief," Nick went on.
"They killed him,
and they want to frame me.
I need your help, Lola.
I know who killed Ann.
At least, I think I know.
But I need time.
There's just one more place I have to visit.
Then I'll be sure.
Can I use your car tonight?"

Lola wasn't listening.
"Blade is dead," she repeated. Her voice was shaky.
"Why does everyone have to die?"

"You're playing with the big boys now," Nick said.
"They'll do anything to save their own skins.
They've got their damn dirty racket,
all those girls, all that dope and the blue movies.
They'll kill anyone who gets in their way.
You....me....Blade....anyone!"

"So they killed Ann," said Lola.
"I knew it."
Nick didn't answer.
He walked to the door.

"Nick, wait!"
Lola ran over to him.
She stood close
and looked up into his eyes.
"Be careful tonight, Nick."
"Sure," he said.
"You're the only one I can trust now,"
she said softly.

They moved slowly together,
looking into each other's eyes,
and then they were kissing
and Nick could taste the smoke in her mouth.
And he wanted that kiss to go on for ever.
But it didn't.

Suddenly Lola pulled away.
"God, you're cold," she said.
"You must have *really* loved her."

Nick turned away.
He shook his head.
"It was….a sort of love…."
He frowned and closed his eyes.
The memory was like a pain —
a pain that wouldn't go away…….

45

An End

*"You're so **cold,** you son of a bitch!" Ann screamed,*
"Why did I ever get mixed up with you?"

She picked up the ashtray.
It was made of glass and shaped like a heart.
She threw it at his head.
It hit the wall,
and smashed into pieces.

Ann burst into tears
and shut herself in the bedroom.
Nick could hear her sobbing
on the other side of the door.
He started to pick up the broken glass.

It was getting worse.
Every time he saw Ann,
it always ended in a fight.
She always drank too much,
and she always ended up in tears.
Nick couldn't stand it.
He couldn't take any more.

Dames, he said to himself —
You can't live with them
and you can't live without them.

Nick went into the bedroom
and sat on the bed next to Ann.
She looked away.

"All I ever wanted," she said,
"was someone to love me.
You don't love me, Nick. You don't care.
You just hang around here.
You don't want what I want.

Her voice was strange and quiet.
She didn't sound drunk any more.
"You should see a doctor," said Nick.

"I don't need a doctor, said Ann.
"That's not what I need.
I just need you to tell me you love me.
That's all Nick.
Just tell me you love me."

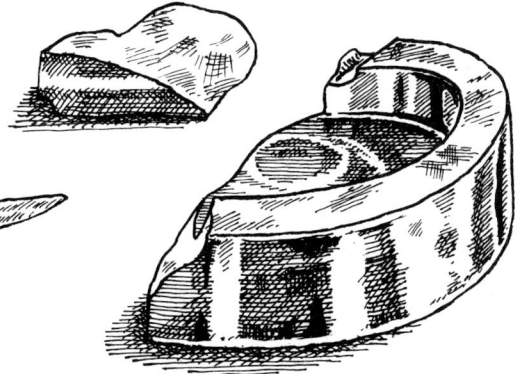

Nick stood up and went to the door.
Ann ran to him and fell to her knees.
She put her arms around his legs
so he couldn't walk.

"Please don't leave me —
please don't go!" she begged.
"If you walk out on me —
I'll kill myself!
I don't want to live —
not without you!"

Nick stood in the doorway,
looking down at her.
He didn't know what to say.
He didn't know what to do.
Ann was crying again,
holding tighter and tighter.
How could he break free?

Ann had tried to kill herself once before —
he'd seen the cuts on her wrist.
Would she really try again?

"You scare me, Ann," Nick murmured.
It was all he could think to say.

He only knew
he had to get away.

The Doctor

Nick got Dr. Mansfield's address
from the book on Lola's desk.
It was a big house
down on Zuma Beach.
Nick knew it well.
He used to take Ann to that beach.

Nick threw Lola's car
along the twisting coast road.
He was angry now.
He couldn't stop thinking about Ann.
He wanted to kill someone,
but he knew he had to keep cool.

Nick got to the beach
and parked the car on the sand.
He splashed sea-water over his shirt.
Then he ran his wet hands through his hair
and over his face.

He went up to the house
and rang the bell.

He started shaking all over.
It was all part of the plan.

A thin old man came to the door
and looked at him.
"Yes?"

"Are you Dr. Mansfield?" Nick said in a shaky voice.
"I need….help…
I need….a shot Doc….a fix…
It's been two days….Doc….I'm dying…"

They stood looking at one another
while the Doctor made up his mind.
He fell for it.
"Come inside," he said.

The house was large and light and clean.
The Doctor was a rich man,
and Nick knew how he made his money.
He sold drugs to people.
People like Rico and Blade Raines.

The Doctor led Nick into his study.
"You shouldn't have come here," he said.
"It's too dangerous.
Blade is a fool."
"Blade is dead," Nick said.
"So is Ann Hammond.
You knew her, didn't you Doc?"

Dr. Mansfield dropped into the chair by his desk.
He sat still for a moment.
Then he opened a drawer
and started to pull out a gun.
Nick moved quickly
and kicked the gun out of his hand.

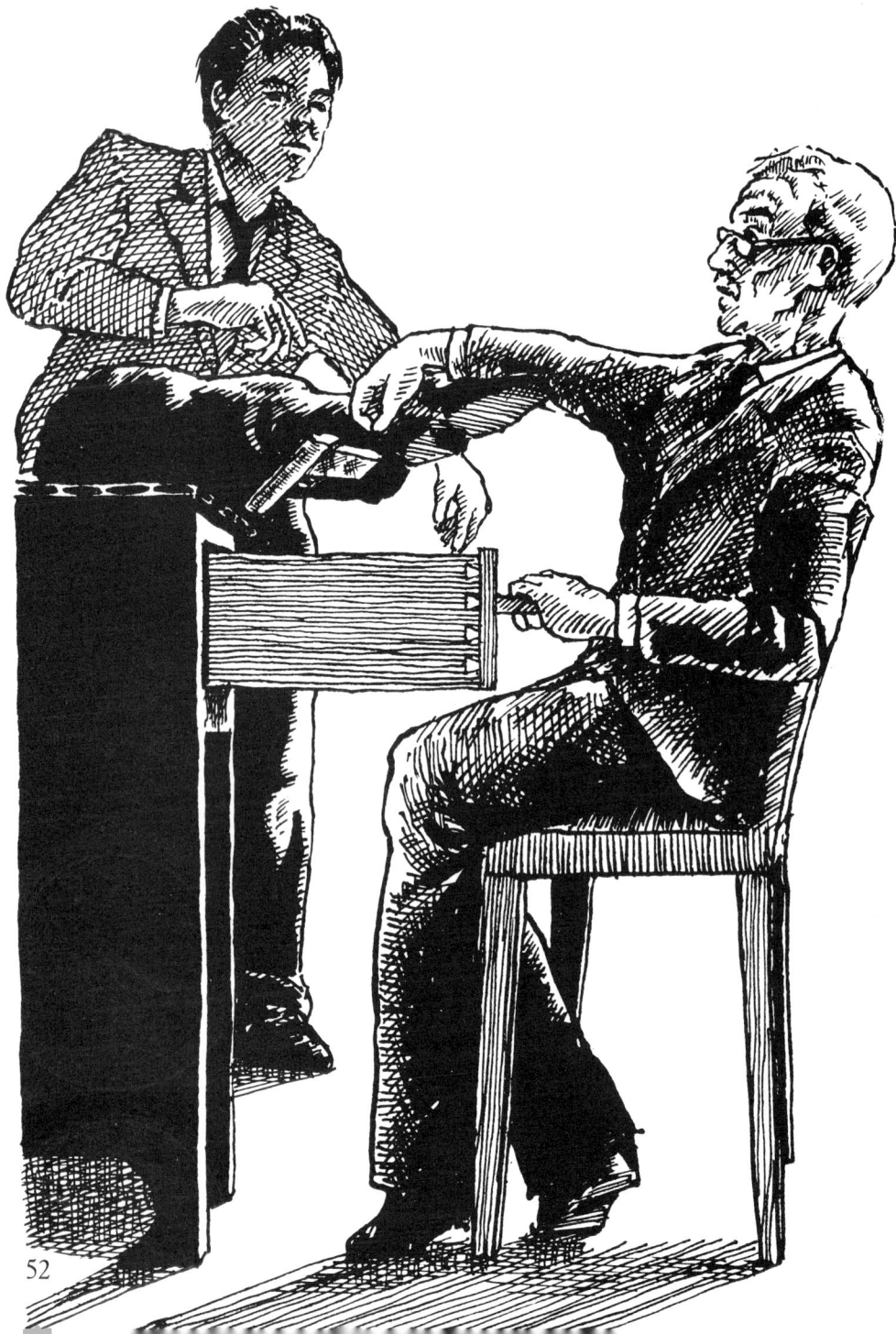

He lifted the Doctor up by his jacket.
He pushed him to the wall
and threw him against it.
The Doctor fell to the floor.

"I talked to the cops today, Doc," Nick said.
"Not your pal The Police Chief,
but *my* pal. A guy named Jack."

"I told him that I didn't kill Blade Raines.
I told him Rico did it.
Then Jack told me about Ann Hammond.
He got the lab tests today.
She was a drug addict.
Someone had been giving her drugs."

The Doctor looked up at Nick.

Nick took the gun from his pocket
and held it to the Doctor's head.
"You've got two minutes, Doc.
Start talking."

True Story

It took more than two minutes,
but Nick got the story out of the Doctor.

Ann worked at *"LOLA'S"*.
The Club had Lola's name on it,
but Rico was the real boss.

Dr. Mansfield went to *"LOLA'S"*.
Sometimes he sold drugs to Rico.
He'd seen Ann there many times —
a beautiful, sad-looking woman.
But they hadn't spoken much,
until the night of the party.

She came up to him
and asked for his help —
she needed a doctor.
They talked.
Ann told him she was hooked on drugs.
She got the stuff from Rico, but he was mean.
He didn't treat her so well.

The Doctor agreed to meet her after the party.
"I felt sorry for her," he said.
"I wanted to help.
I think I was a little in love with her."

When they met later,
the Doctor knew he'd made a big mistake.
Ann wanted his help to get *more* drugs.
She didn't want to kick the habit at all.
She begged him for a fix.
But the Doctor didn't have any drugs with him.
He'd only come to help her.
Ann went wild.
She flew into a rage,
and came at him with a knife.

The Doctor grabbed her arm
and twisted it behind her back.
He got the knife from her,
but she kept hitting out and punching him.

He had his arms around her.
He was trying to hold her still,
but they stumbled and fell.
Ann screamed.
Her body jerked once.
Then she lay still.

He was still holding on to the knife,
and the blade was deep in her back.

He dragged her to the sofa,
but there was nothing he could do.
She died in his arms.

The Doctor was in tears.

"I wanted to help her.
I didn't want her to die...."

Nick picked up the phone.
He got through to Jack.

"It's Nick. I'm down at Zuma Beach.
I'm with an old man.
He's got a story for you.
About Ann Hammond...."

"Yes. Sure, Jack. I'll wait till you get here."

Nick hung up.

A Stab in the Heart

Nick was back at *"LOLA'S"*.
He was half-way down a bottle of scotch.

"Why do I feel so bad?" he said.
"I got the killer.
Rico and The Police Chief are in jail.
I saved you Lola….
So why do I feel so bad?"

Lola went over and touched his hand.
"It's a big bad world, Nick."

"Ann must have been so alone," Nick went on.
"Why did it happen?"

"Like I told you before," said Lola, bitterly.
"It's a man's world.
Men chew you up
and they spit you out."

She tried to take the bottle away,
but Nick held on to it.

"I used to be a top reporter," he said.
"*Now* look at me —
just another drunk in a bar."

He drank another scotch.
Then another.

Nick turned to Lola.
"I'm going to tell you….
I never told anyone….till now.
I knew Ann six years ago."

"I guessed," said Lola.

"We were together for a year," Nick went on,
"but it didn't work.
I walked out on her.
I never saw her again.

"Ann tried to kill herself.
All those scars and the bracelets….remember?
She wanted to die —
the old Doc just helped her to do it.
He held the knife,
but she was already dying.
She had been for years.

"We killed her between us," said Nick slowly.
"The Doc and me.
He stabbed her in the back,
and I stabbed her in the heart."